Balancing the Act
Juggling Parenthood and Career

Table of Contents

Chapter 1. Introduction

Ever wondered how to simultaneously chase your professional passions while being a full-fledged parent? In this exceptional Special Report, "Balancing the Act: Juggling Parenthood and Career," we delve into the heart of this maze, offering compassionate advice, evidence-based strategies, and real-life stories to inspire you. Excitingly, we've blended just the right amount of motivation and practical knowledge to give you the best of both worlds. Unlock the secret to manage time, overcome challenges, and indeed, excel at both— parenthood and career, while maintaining your sanity. This report isn't merely a guide, it's a ticket to discovering a new you, promising a life that harmonizes your love for work with the responsibilities and joys of parenting. What's more? It's a delightful journey waiting to be embarked on, right at the flip of a page. Get fueled for this empowering journey and own the key to achieving the ultimate work-life balance. Equip yourself with this report now and master the art of juggling!

Chapter 2. Understanding the Challenge: Parenthood Vs. Career

The thrill of cracking a career milestone, the fluttering joy of watching your child take their first step - these sentiments are sweet in their unique ways and equally challenging to manage under the same roof. To familiarize ourselves with the true extent of this conundrum, it's important to delve into the core challenges that could pose as roadblocks.

2.1. Understanding The Dual Role

When you are a professional as well as a parent, you are essentially playing dual roles. One requires you to be focused, ambitious, aggressive and the other calls for compassion, patience, and selflessness. Balancing these diverse roles can often seem like a daunting task. Each role comes with its obligations, each demanding its share of time. As a result, the constant shift between these roles can lead to overwhelming stress and anxiety.

2.2. The Time Constraint

Arguably, time is the most significant mutual asset required by both professional and parental roles. Both claim a major share of your 24-hour day. While professional commitments might engage you in long hours of work, parenting means being available for your children anytime they need you. And, unfortunately, the exigencies of one often spill into the time allocated for the other, disrupting the delicate balance. How can one possibly manage such a constrictively tight schedule?

2.3. The Quest for Perfection

In a world obsessed with picture-perfect portrayals, there's immense pressure to be a 'perfect' professional and a 'perfect' parent. This constant chase toward perfection takes a tremendous toll on mental health. What contributes to this strain is the gnawing guilt that you're falling short in one role when you're succeeding in the other. It's crucial to understand that it's okay not to be perfect all the time, and instead, concentrate on doing your best in either role.

2.4. The Problem of Presence

In professional settings, 'presence' could mean active participation in meetings, while in parenting, it might refer to being mentally and physically available for your children. Both roles necessitate your full attention, and the challenge lies in managing not to let your attention from one role encroach the other. It's quite a challenge to master the art of 'presence' amidst the hustle.

2.5. Handling the Emotional Rollercoaster

As a parent, the emotional connection that ties you to your child is naturally strong and almost instinctual. It requires care, nurture, and immense patience. In stark contrast, the professional sphere calls for rational and strategic thinking, often devoid of emotions. The constant tug between the emotional and rational, the heart and the mind, can create a tumultuous internal conflict that might be challenging to resolve.

Having understood the core challenges, it's useful to know that being both a dedicated professional and a devoted parent isn't an impossible feat. It rather requires effective strategizing, adapting, and constant learning. As the journey unfolds, it's essential to realize that the secret lies in embracing the chaos, the noise, and the mess - transforming them into coordinated symphonies. The magic unfolds when you harmonize these seemingly contrasting melodies into a concert of your choice - creating beautiful music that resonates with your unique life tune.

In the following sections, we'll delve deeper into strategies to tackle these challenges head-on. From managing time effectively to silencing the perfectionist within, from juggling presence across these roles to dealing with emotional upheavals – we will explore it all! As the chronicles of numerous successful career parents have demonstrated, while it might seem like an uphill task, it's a journey worth climbing. It is here you'll understand that you don't have to pick a side in the Parenting Vs. Career debate, you can instead carve your pathway - blending the best of both worlds with a little bit of ingenuity and a lot of patience.

Chapter 3. Realigning Your Goals: Setting Priorities Straight

It's rare for any task to begin without establishing goals. Whether it's a simple activity like sewing a button or an extensive project like building a rocket, your objective needs to be defined. Similarly, for the titanic task of balancing your career with parenthood, delineating your priorities is the first demanding but necessary step.

3.1. Defining Goals: The Initial Step

Listing down your aspirations can present a clear vision of what you're striving to achieve. Start by listing all your ambitions - both career and family related. Remember to focus on what you truly desire, not what is expected of you by society or your acquaintances. At this stage, it would help to reflect on where you see yourself in a few years regarding both your personal and professional life. Are you aiming for a promotion or looking forward to achieving a particular life-work balance?

3.2. Identifying Priorities: The Crux of the Matter

It is essential to categorize your goals and decide which ones are non-negotiable and which ones you're willing to put on hold. This categorization can be based on different parameters like your financial stability, the age of your children, or the demands of your job. Comparing the importance of different goals may lead to some restructuring of your life and time allocation.

3.3. The Gravity of Financial Goals

While detailing your aspirations, financial considerations will inevitably come into play. Do you aim to earn a specific sum by a certain age? Is your goal to establish financial security for your children's future? Be honest about your ambitions but also realistic. Understanding if these goals stand at the crux could greatly influence your decision about career advancement versus parenting responsibilities.

3.4. The Subtlety of Emotional Goals

Your emotional goals are as important as your financial ones. Yearning for deeper satisfaction at work, or hoping for stronger bonds with your children – these can also become guiding factors. These aspirations should be weighed equally against responsibilities like working extra hours or assisting your children in their school projects.

3.5. Of Fluid Goals and Changing Priorities

An element often overlooked is the fluidity of goals and priorities. Human desires and aspirations are dynamic, and this fluidity should be incorporated into your plan. Your job might take a backseat when your child is young, but as they grow and become more independent, you may wish to rekindle your past career objectives. Being open to such changes can allow you a more harmonious alignment between parenthood and career.

3.6. Piecing It Together: Formulating a Strategy

If the initial steps were about laying the groundwork, piecing it together signifies the process of structuring your days, weeks, and even years to move towards your goals. It includes evaluating your time, resources, and commitments against the backdrop of your goals. It could mean re-negotiating household responsibilities with your partner, or it may lead to finding new ways to manage your time more efficiently.

3.7. Develop a Flexible Routine

Once your priorities have been aligned to your goals, it's time to develop a manageable routine. Routines provide a sense of order and predictability that can reduce stress. However, ensure your schedule possesses an element of flexibility to tackle unforeseen situations or changes in priorities.

3.8. Incorporating Self-care

With the intense focus on achieving a careful balance between parenthood and career, one aspect professionals often overlook is self-care. In your pursuit of success in both spheres, don't forget your wellbeing. Incorporate time for rest, relaxation, and hobbies in your routine.

In conclusion, striking the perfect balance between work and parenthood is an art. It requires introspection, planning, flexibility, and most importantly, patience. By setting your goals straight and aligning your priorities correctly, you can embark on a fulfilling journey of successful parenting whilst fulfilling your professional ambitions, resulting in an accomplished and balanced life.

Chapter 4. Time Management: Smarter Ways to Divide and Conquer

Effective time management begins with gaining insight into your typical workday and identifying time thieves. In doing so, you gain control of your schedule, enabling you to reach a balance between work and parenthood. To help guide you through this process, we will explore time management principles, smart tricks, and tools that should be integrated into your everyday life, with practical examples for better understanding.

4.1. Principle One: Identify your Time Thieves

Time thieves are those seemingly harmless activities, distractions, or interruptions that steal your time. They can be physical, such as clutter on your desk or countless emails that aimlessly wander into your inbox. They can also be mental, like anxiety or a lack of focus. Identifying your time thieves is the first step toward effective time management.

For instance, it could be smartphone notifications that distract you or frequent interruptions from colleagues. As a parent, maybe it's the constant need to clean up after your children, or perhaps constantly checking your work emails even during off-hours. Take one week to note down all activities that take hours from your day but don't contribute to your productivity, label them as your time thieves, and then deliberate on strategies to minimize or eliminate them.

4.2. Principle Two: Prioritize your Tasks

Knowing your priorities is key to achieving balance between parenthood and career. Establish clear work and home priorities, and stick to them. Use the Eisenhower Decision Matrix to help you identify tasks based on their urgency and importance.

The matrix consists of four quadrants:

1. Urgent and important

2. Important, but not urgent

3. Urgent, but not important

4. Not urgent, not important

Use this tool to schedule your tasks into these categories, thereby helping you to visualize where your attention should be. For example, meeting a project deadline is both important and urgent, while going grocery shopping is urgent but not necessarily important (you can delegate this to someone else or order online). The key is knowing how to delegate less important tasks whenever possible, and focusing your energy on what truly matters.

4.3. Tool One: Use Technological Tools

Integrating time-management applications into your routine can help automate or streamline your tasks. Tools like Asana, Trello, or Google Calendar can help manage your work and personal tasks seamlessly. These tools offer features such as task tracking, deadlines, collaborative space, and reminders. Mastering these tools can help free up time and ensure you're focused on your priority tasks.

4.4. Principle Three: Set Boundaries and Learn to Say No

Saying no can be difficult, especially when it feels like everything on your plate is important. However, taking on too much can lead to stress, making you less efficient. Learn to say no to unnecessary meetings, social commitments, or extra tasks that contribute to your time thieves.

At home, create a work-free zone or time. Set boundaries with your children or partner, explaining when you'd be available and when you need to focus on work. This helps your family understand your needs and commitments, creating a healthier work-life balance.

4.5. Time Management Tips for Parents

Parenthood comes with unpredictable and demanding tasks. Children require your attention and care, making time management a bit more complex. Here are some tips aimed towards parents:

- **Create Routines:** Children thrive on predictability. Create daily or weekly routines for both yourself and your children. It gives them a sense of security and helps you plan your day.

- **Batching:** Combine similar tasks to increase your productivity. For instance, cook meals in large quantities and freeze for the rest of the week. At work, try batching emails or phone calls instead of addressing them as they come.

- **Delegate:** Enlist help when possible. Whether it's asking your spouse to take over bedtime duties, hiring a babysitter, or delegating tasks to your team members at work. You don't have to do it all alone.

This chapter aims to provide you with valuable strategies to improve your time management skills. Remember, though, this is a journey. Take small steps, and gradually incorporate these principles and tools into your life. Over time, you will find a rhythm that works for you, providing you with the balance you seek between your career and parenthood.

Chapter 5. The Art of Delegation: Maximizing Your Resources

Delegating is an art form as much as it is a practical skill. Mastering it involves understanding the strengths and weaknesses of your team—the human resources at your disposal—as well as your own limitations. Delegation, when implemented effectively, can lead to increased productivity, enhanced team dynamics, skill development, and better work life balance. For parents juggling career obligations and familial responsibilities, understanding how to delegate can be a game-changer.

5.1. The Psychology of Delegation

The idea of delegating tasks is often met with resistance. Fear of losing control, fear of being perceived as lazy, or the misconception that one can handle all responsibilities on their own are some of the psychological barriers that deter individuals from effective delegation. Removing these misconceptions and fears is paramount to becoming effective at delegation. Remember, it isn't a reflection of inability or laziness, but rather a sign of a mature, effective leader who knows how to make efficient use of resources.

5.2. Harness the Power of Delegation

Delegation done right can lead to several benefits, both on a personal and professional level. It can lead to improved productivity, increased work satisfaction, enhanced time management, reduced stress levels, and accelerated career growth. Additionally, it gives team members the opportunity to develop new skills, widen their experience, and enhance their performance. And while all this happens at work, at home, it allows for more quality family time and less burnout.

5.3. Attributes of Effective Delegation

Effective delegation is an intricate balance of trust, respect, and support. It involves assigning tasks based on individual capabilities and potential, not just piling work on anyone who is available. Good leaders delegate by empowering their team members, fostering an environment conducive to growth and learning, and showing faith in their team's abilities.

5.4. The Delegation Process

Successful delegation follows a clear process:

1. Identify the tasks
2. Decide who the task should go to
3. Explain why they are chosen
4. Clearly convey expectations
5. Provide adequate resources
6. Set milestones and deadlines
7. Regularly review and provide feedback
8. Recognize and appreciate their work

Following this process can help you delegate tasks successfully without causing confusion or frustration.

5.5. Enhancing Your Delegation Skills

If delegation feels like a struggle, don't lose hope. With dedication and practice, anyone can learn to delegate effectively. First, accept that you cannot do everything and that delegation is a necessity. Start by practicing with small tasks, observe the outcomes, tweak your approach, and gradually advance to larger, more significant responsibilities. Gather feedback, constantly improve and remember: the goal is to nurture your team and free up your time for essential tasks.

5.6. Delegation at Home

Delegation isn't solely a workplace strategy. It can also be applied effectively at home. From involving kids in simple household chores to sharing responsibilities with your spouse, delegation fosters a sense of teamwork and mutual accountability. It allows parents to manage their time better and also gives children a sense of responsibility and involvement.

5.7. Dealing with Delegation Mishaps

Despite careful planning and implementation, things can go wrong. When they do, it's crucial to approach the situation with understanding and empathy. Handle it as a learning opportunity, rather than resorting to blame. Correct the course, offer support, and ensure learning was facilitated from the experience.

Mastering the art of delegation isn't a swift process. It requires patience, persistence and constantly honing and adjusting your approach to get it right. But once you do, it's the ticket to creating a more balanced and fulfilling personal life while nurturing a high-performance professional environment. For parents juggling their career and family life, it's no less than a superpower.

5.8. Conclusion

Being an effective delegate isn't about passing off work. It's about maximizing your resources—those valuable human resources around you—to create the most productive, efficient, and effective outcomes possible. Whether you're delegating a project at work or assigning chores at home, the concept remains the same: it's about trust, efficiency, and empowerment.

When you master the art of delegation, you create a supportive, trusting environment where everyone's skills are utilized to their best potential. You free up time in your schedule, time that can be better used by being with family, pursuing personal interests, or working on high-value tasks that only you can do. Unlock the power of delegation and discover a newfound sense of balance in your professional and personal life.

Chapter 6. Surviving Guilt: Removing the Parenting Vs. Professional Tag

Many parents grapple with a nagging feeling of guilt that inspires thoughts of self-doubt. They are constantly torn between the demands of their professional commitments and the unconditional nurturance that parenting involves. Indeed, the Parenting Vs. Professional tag is a perceived conflict that many of us struggle with.

6.1. Understanding Guilt

Guilt is an emotional response that arises when we perceive that we have failed to meet our own or society's expectations. When it comes to juggling parenthood and your career, guilt can take various forms. You might feel guilty for not spending enough time with your children, for not contributing sufficiently to a team project at work, or even for not managing to keep your house in perfect order. But guilt, in reality, is your profound consciousness of connection, responsibility, and love towards each role you play.

Understand that guilt isn't necessarily a negative emotion; we just have to understand and manage it better. It's important to perceive guilt as an indicator that some area in your life requires more attention or a different approach.

6.2. Overcoming Guilt

The first step to overcoming guilt is acknowledging it. Admit to yourself that you're feeling guilty. This honest self-reflection is crucial, and it's okay to feel this way. It's a part of the journey, and this acknowledgment is the first step towards finding a solution.

Write down your feelings, challenge them, and question their validity.

Next, strive for 'balance' and not 'perfection.' The idea of being a perfect parent or a flawless professional is a myth. Balance requires understanding your capabilities, recognizing your limitations, and creating a harmonious environment for yourself where you feel content.

6.3. Scheduling and Bound Management

Creating a definitive schedule can miraculously alchemize your time into seemingly more hours. Delineate professional and personal hours in a day, and stick to the plan rigidly. Set boundaries for your work and carve out exclusive leisure time for your family. Try to be fully present in whatever you do and avoid multitasking.

Also, effective communication with your partner, your children, and your colleagues will help in balancing expectations. Convey your priorities, sharing your struggles without hesitation. People around you are more accommodating and understanding than you might think.

6.4. Emotional Self-Care

With an active professional life and a bustling home, it's common to lose touch with your well-being. Guilt tends to increase if you're already feeling emotionally exhausted. Prioritize self-care to manage these feelings better. A well-rested mind can think clearly, make better decisions, and, most importantly, stay positive.

A little attention to exercise, good rest, and a balanced diet can boost your energy levels. Journaling, meditation, mindfulness exercises can also act as channels to vent your feelings, leading to a healthier mindset.

6.5. Seeking Professional Help

There is absolutely nothing wrong in seeking professional help if guilt starts to overwhelm you. Therapists and psychologists can provide a fresh perspective, helping you navigate your feelings in a more structured and objective way. They can arm you with strategies to tackle situations that trigger guilt.

6.6. The Power of Networking

Connecting with other parents who juggle their careers and parenthood can be a valuable resource. It allows for a mutual exchange of experiences, advice, empathy, and support. Hearing about the trials, tribulations, and triumphs of others can reassure you that you're not alone, and the feelings of guilt you experience are very common.

6.7. Using Positive Affirmations

Positive affirmations can help you combat recurring feelings of guilt. Repeating phrases like "I am doing my best," "I am enough," or "My career and my family are equally important," helps reinforce positive self-images and attitudes.

In conclusion, changing your mindset, managing your time, taking care of yourself emotionally, seeking professional help, networking with fellow parents, and using positive affirmations are the keys to keeping guilt at bay. Every person's situation is unique, and what works for one may not work for all. Therefore, it's important to customize these strategies and incorporate them into your life based on your personal needs and circumstances.

The ultimate goal is not to become a guilt-free parent or professional, but to manage that guilt to the point where it no longer commands you. Every struggle you face is merely a sign of your beautiful evolution as a parent and professional. And remember, in this juggling act, you're not alone. Let's toss guilt aside, and forge ahead on this spectacular journey to achieving a balanced life!

Chapter 7. Stress Management: Keeping Your Cool Amid Chaos

Today's fast-paced world can often feel like it's teeming with demands that require attention and action. Professional deadlines vie for your attention, while your child's needs equally summon you-- pulling you in two distinct directions that often feels overwhelming. This chaos, if poorly managed, can lead to enormous stress, affecting both your productivity and your relationships.

However, fear not! There's an arsenal of strategies that can aid in navigating this tumultuous terrain with grace and poise. In attempting to unravel the mystery of stress management, we will employ a three-fold approach— understanding stress, identifying your stressors, and learning stress management techniques.

7.1. Understanding Stress

Stress is essentially a physical response. It is our body's way of responding to any kind of demand or threat. When we sense danger, whether it's real or perceived, the body's defenses kick in through a rapid, automatic process known as the "fight-or-flight" reaction, or the stress response.

Though often seen in a negative light, stress isn't always bad. In manageable doses, stress can help you perform under pressure and motivate you to put forth your best effort. But when you're constantly in emergency mode, your mind and body can pay the price.

7.2. Identifying Your Stressors

Recognizing the triggers or sources of stress (stressors) is the first critical step in stress management. Because the sources of stress are different for everyone, it's essential to understand what's causing your stress.

Begin by making a list of significant events, either at work or home, which make you feel anxious or stressed. This could range from tight deadlines at work to your child's school projects or health conditions. Write down how each event makes you feel and why. Keep record—it will help you understand patterns in your stress and aid in developing ideas for managing it.

7.3. Techniques for Stress Management

Once you've started identifying your stressors, you can begin to explore various stress management techniques. These strategies are meant to equip you with skills to maintain your composure amidst the chaos:

7.4. Mindful Breathing

Research indicates that focusing on the physical act of breathing can assist in providing a diversion from the anxieties of your mind, thereby reducing stress. During particularly tense moments, try taking slow, deep belly breaths in through your nose, pause, then slowly release the breath out through your mouth. Repeating this for a few minutes can help to alter your stress response and promote relaxation.

7.5. The Power of Positive Affirmations

Positive affirmations can be a powerful antidote to stress. These are positive statements or phrases that you repeat to yourself to combat negative thoughts or feelings. Practice using positive affirmations daily, specifying them to your particular stressors. For example, if being away from your child while at work stresses you, your affirmation could be, "My child is safe and happy. I can focus on my work."

7.6. Exercise Regularly

Exercise is a well-known stress reducer. It increases the production of "feel-good" chemicals in your brain, like endorphins, and can help distract you from daily worries. It doesn't have to be a strenuous workout—a brisk walk, yoga, or any physical activity can act as a powerful stress reliever.

7.7. Maintain a Balanced Diet

Our dietary habits significantly impact our ability to manage stress. Consuming a diet high in processed foods, caffeine, and sugar can exacerbate feelings of stress. On the other hand, a diet rich in vegetables, fruits, lean proteins, and whole grains can help provide the necessary nutrients your body needs to handle stress.

7.8. Establish Healthy Boundaries

Learn to say "no" and set boundaries both at work and at home. While it can be challenging, it's necessary for managing stress. Remember—you're only human, and it's okay to turn down additional tasks if they overload your capacity.

In conclusion, managing stress is integral when juggling parenthood and a career. The chaos will invariably present itself, but with apt stress management strategies, it will become just another aspect of life that you can tackle with ease. Remember, the goal isn't to eliminate all stress but rather to create a balanced response to stressors. With time, patience, and regular practice, these techniques can help mitigate the effects of stress, enabling you to lead a healthy and balanced life in all aspects. It all starts with a single step—take yours today.

Chapter 8. Building a Support Network: Finding Your Tribe

It's often said that it takes a village to raise a child, and that's especially the case when you are juggling the demands of a career with the responsibilities of parenthood. A strong support network can make all the difference in your ability to thrive in both areas of your life. Let's delve into how you can build such a network and find your tribe.

There might be a tendency to believe that this journey is about shouldering the mighty world alone, a precursor to success. That's far from the truth. Your tribe, your support network, is your backbone, and here's why:

Independence does not mean isolation. It means acknowledging the presence of others in your path, leaning on them for support, and reciprocating when they need you. The most empowered individuals understand the importance of seeking help and offering it, thereby forming robust connections.

8.1. The Importance of a Support Network

In the rigors of baby peals and boardroom presentations, the significance of a support network often gets overshadowed. However, the role it plays is fundamentally transformational. A sturdy network of like-minded or empathetic individuals can be quite a boon for busy parents.

A support network doesn't just offer a helping hand during tough times. It's a community that helps you grow and flourish in your personal and professional life, sharing meaningful experiences, disbursing advice, imparting wisdom, and instigating personal growth.

When you're juggling multiple demands, the support from those who understand your struggles can help keep you motivated and on top of things. Moreover, a support network can also provide practical assistance. For instance, someone in your network may be able to recommend good daycare facilities or possible babysitters. Or somebody else could provide mentorship and guidance for your professional growth.

8.2. Identifying Who Your Tribe Will Be

Your tribe comprises handpicked individuals who understand your struggles, are generous with advice, and who believe in you. They're your go-to people in times of joy or tribulation. Practicality dictates that your tribe should include people who can give you insights into different aspects of your life.

For a balance between parenthood and your career, consider forming a tribe that includes:

1. Fellow parents

2. Career mentors

3. Friends who are also balancing work and parenting

4. Family members

These different perspectives will ensure that advice you receive is well-rounded, and it caters to diverse problem areas. For instance, fellow parents can give you practical advice based on their experiences. Career mentors can help you advance in your professional roles.

8.3. Strategies to Build Your Support Network

Building a strong support network isn't something that happens overnight, but it's absolutely worth the investment of time and energy. Here are some strategic steps to embarking on this journey.

1. Reach Out:

Start by identifying people around you who might be a good fit for your support network. Recognize and seek connections at your workplace, parent groups, or social networking sites geared toward working parents. Initiate communications with openness and candidness.

1. Be Reciprocal:

Building a support network is not just about taking, but giving as well. Be there for your tribe. Show up when they need you and offer your unique skills and supports to them as well. Reciprocity is at the heart of any healthy relationship.

1. Maintain Consistent Communication:

Stay in regular touch with your support network, even during less stressful periods. Regular check-ins, updates, and get-togethers can strengthen these bonds.

1. Foster Close Connections:

Deeper connections often mean more reliable support. Foster these deeper relationships by sharing honest sentiments about your struggles and successes.

8.4. Leveraging Technology for Networking

Technology can play a crucial role in building and maintaining your support network. Social media platforms can be useful tools to connect with other working parents and find mentorship opportunities. Online groups and forums can also provide a platform to share tips, advice, and support.

Yet, clicking the 'add friend' button doesn't make someone part of your tribe automatically. Nurture digital relationships with as much care as you nurture in-person connections. Genuine conversations, active participation, and empathy go a long way in bolstering your online support network.

Building a support network doesn't happen instantly. It requires energy, time, empathy, and consistent effort. But each step you take toward nurturing your tribe brings you closer to finding that balance between parenthood and your career. So don't discount this important strategy, and remember — you're investing not just in your well-being, but also in your success.

Chapter 9. Taking Care of You: Self-care in the Midst of Juggling

Often, amid a whirlwind of professional commitments and parenting chores, your own needs may slip between the cracks. Yet, remembering to take care of yourself is not just invaluable for your personal well-being but also critical in fulfilling your roles as both a parent and a professional. In this chapter, we explore various strategies aimed at fostering self-care while you seamlessly juggle your dual responsibilities.

9.1. Understanding the Importance of Self-Care

Self-care is much more than the occasional indulgence – it is a continuous process of engaging in activities that rejuvenate your mental, physical, and emotional wellbeing. When immersed in work or caring for your children, you may overlook the subtle signals of your body and mind asking for rest. Understanding the importance of self-care is the first step in nurturing yourself.

Scientific research reveals that consistent self-care practices can significantly reduce stress and anxiety, improve physical health, enhance self-esteem, and boost overall happiness and satisfaction. More importantly, when you regularly attend to your needs, you are better equipped to meet the demands of your work and family life.

9.2. Setting Personal Boundaries

Establishing personal boundaries is a powerful self-care tool, vital in striking an ideal work-life balance. These boundaries could be related to your time, your emotional health, or even your personal space. Clearly communicating these boundaries to those around you, including your family and colleagues, is essential.

Remember, setting boundaries isn't about distancing yourself from your responsibilities. Rather, it's about defining your personal limits to protect your wellbeing. Effective boundary setting helps in avoiding burnout and keeps you mentally fresh and physically active.

9.3. Prioritizing Physical Health

Maintaining physical well-being is a significant aspect of self-care. Constant shuttling between parent-teacher meetings, client presentations, and the routine, yet demanding, household chores can take a toll on your health.

Exercise	Benefits
Walking	Boosts physical fitness, aids in weight management
Yoga and Meditation	Relieves stress, enhances flexibility, improves concentration
Regular Health Check-ups	Detects potential health issues early, enables timely treatment
Balanced Diet	Provides necessary nutrition, increases immunity, keeps diseases at bay
Adequate Rest	Restores energy, enhances productivity, improves mood

Ensure you make time to care for your physical health. Whether it's a brisk walk, a calming yoga sequence, or simply getting adequate sleep, make sure these aspects become an integral part of your routine.

9.4. Emotional Care: Embrace your Feelings

Balancing a career and parenthood can often be emotionally challenging. Accepting that it is entirely normal to experience a vast range of emotions — from accomplishment to complete overwhelm — is crucial for self-care.

Connecting with your feelings can be as simple as jotting down your thoughts in a journal or sharing your day's experiences with a close friend. Equally important is seeking professional help if you feel persistently low. There's no shame in accessing counseling or therapy: it's merely a way of ensuring your emotional wellbeing, just as you'd seek a doctor's help for physical ailments.

9.5. Cultivating a Hobby

Engaging in a hobby you enjoy serves as a delightful break from your career and parenting duties. This can rekindle your sense of self beyond being a professional or a parent. Be it gardening, reading, painting, or learning a musical instrument, devoting time to your hobby can act as a powerful stress buster, ultimately promoting joy and fulfillment.

9.6. Mindfulness: The Power of the Present

Mindfulness, the act of being consciously present in the moment, has been lauded across various scientific studies for its numerous benefits, including reducing stress, increasing focus, and enabling a healthier relationship with one's self and others.

Here are a few simple ways to incorporate mindfulness into your day-to-day life:

- Spend a few minutes every day focusing on your breath.

- Engage completely when playing with your children or when unwinding after work.

- Bring attention to the sensations while savoring your meals, or during a leisurely walk.

Over time, mindfulness can help you respond more calmly to the myriad challenges of balancing work and parenthood, paving the way for a more resilient, balanced you.

In essence, self-care isn't a luxury, it's a necessity. The hustle and bustle of life won't pause, but you have the discretion to make a conscious choice: to take a moment for yourself each day. We hope the strategies shared here serve as a beacon guiding you towards a harmonious blend of work, parenting, and heedful self-care. In the end, it's all about nurturing yourself so you can continue nurturing the various aspects of your life with love, patience, and dynamism.

Chapter 10. Real-Life Lessons: Stories from Successful Parent-Professionals

As we venture into the realm of work-life balance, we begin by dipping our toes into the life experiences of successful parent-professionals, people who have beautifully mastered the art of juggling. Their stories, fraught with challenges, yet filled to the brim with triumphs and immense satisfaction, are spread out before us like an open book—inviting us to learn, adopt, edify, and most importantly, believe!

10.1. Time Management Strategies from a Top Entrepreneur

Daniel, an entrepreneur and a father of two, shares his secret of effective time management. He believes that "Time is like money; it needs to be invested wisely." Daniel works by the 'Power of Block Scheduling' method. He dedicates fixed hours for work and parenting. He advocates that one should endeavor to optimize focus during the assigned time slots to accomplish tasks efficiently without compromising quality—whether it's a professional assignment or tucking in your kid. By doing so, Daniel ensures dedicated attention to each aspect of his life, without one bleeding into the other.

10.2. How to Separate Work from Home: A Fortune 500 CEO's Insights

Up next is Angela, a Fortune 500 CEO and a mother of four. Her mantra is "Separate to Integrate." She emphasizes a clear work-home demarcation to ensure both worlds don't collide. She recommends setting clear, communicated boundaries, like fixed work hours and unplugged family times. This strategy has worked wonders for her as she never misses an executive meeting nor her kid's PTA meeting. Angela claims that this separation strategy adds clarity, enhances performance, and boosts one's ability to multitask.

10.3. Overcoming Guilt – Lessons from a Surgeon

Then we have Dr. Amelia, a renowned cardiothoracic surgeon in her field and a dedicated mother of twins, her secret being "guilt management." She shares how initially, she was overwhelmed by the guilt of not being there enough for her children. But then, she developed a personalized coping strategy—embracing that guilt was just a feeling, not a fact. She chose quality over quantity, making sure the time with her kids carried deep emotional value. So, whether it was reading them a bedtime story or a shared ice cream date, she ensured these moments were not only special but also memorable.

10.4. Patience Is Key: An Educator's Tale

Meet Jeremy, a high school principal, and a single dad. His life is replete with myriad tasks—handling school affairs, attending to his children, and house chores. His personal and professional roles often intertwined, leading to frustration. After a crucial self-realization, Jeremy concluded, "Patience, not pace determines success." He started dedicating time to mindful practices including meditation and yoga which improved his patience significantly. The result was—he was less agitated, more focused, and carried a more positive persona at work and home.

10.5. Building emotional resilience: Insights from a Marine Veteran

Our next inspiration comes from Hannah, a Marine veteran turned software engineer, and a mother. She decodes the essence of emotional resilience in managing career and parenthood: "Always improvise, adapt, and overcome." Life threw different challenges at her, from grueling deployments to demanding software releases. But every stressor only strengthened her emotional resolve. In parenthood, she used these lessons, making herself an imperturbable anchor in her family. Role reconciliation was her modus operandi: she ceased to picture work and family responsibilities as battling forces, instead, viewed them as complementing roles that make herself complete.

10.6. Upholding Passion & Positivity: A Celebrity Chef Turns the Heat

Our final epicure of wisdom is celebrity chef and TV presenter Marco, who, along with cooking mouth-watering cuisines, manages his roles as a father of three, with deftness and flair. He emphasizes that passion and positivity are the key ingredients. Marco's zest for his profession and an undying love for his family fuel him. Even amidst the chaos, he finds joy—thus making the journey as delightful as the goal. For him, work and parenting are not burdens that he juggles, but loves that he balances.

By examining the journeys of these diverse individuals, we can deduce that unique, bespoke strategies work for each one of them. The common denominators are effective time management, the art of separation, dealing with guilt, patience, emotional resilience, and maintaining passion and positivity.

As we stitch together their stories, we cannot help but notice that these successful parent-professionals didn't attain a perfect work-life balance overnight. It was an iterative process of trial and error. They often fell, learned, adapted, and then sprang back to life—stronger, better, and more confident.

Undeniably, these real-life lessons sow the seeds of resilience, patience, and smart work within us. With careful nurturing, they can give rise to robust strategies tailored to your beautiful, chaotic, rewarding life as a parent-professional. As we learn from these masters, we discover that your personal journey towards a balanced life is just a few tweaks away— tweaks that this guide will help you make!

Chapter 11. Embracing the Balance: Celebrating Success in Work and Parenting

Regardless of how organized and efficient you are, striking the perfect balance between your professional pursuits and parenting duties is no easy task. It's like walking on a tightrope, where acquiescence to one side might lead to the unsettling tremors on the other. However, the world is full of individuals who have mastered this act, fueling their career aspirations, while simultaneously being hands-on parents, nurturing their offspring lovingly and efficiently. Glancing at their celebration of triumphs in both spheres, we can glean valuable insights and strategies to integrate into our pursuit of harmonizing work and parenting.

11.1. Actionable Steps: Mastering the Balance

Having a clear vision and actionable steps can significantly expedite your journey towards achieving balance between career aspirations and parenting responsibilities.

1. Daily To-Do Lists: Start each day by creating a to-do list, prioritizing activities based on their urgency and importance. Organizing your day's tasks helps in efficiently allocating time and energy.

2. Time Management: Implement a schedule that accommodates both work responsibilities and parenting duties. Consider start and end times for a workday, time set aside for kids' activities, personal relaxation, and family time.

3. Set Boundaries: Sharing professional pursuits and familial roles

with your partner can ease the pressure. Also, ensure boundaries are maintained between work timing and family time.

4. Use Technology: Make use of available technology to become more organized. Digital calendars, reminder apps, virtual assistants, all can help keep track and manage time effectively.

It is important to remember that this balance does not represent an ideal to be achieved. Instead, it is a continuous process, involving constant adjustments and readjustments. It involves embracing this ebb and flow with grace and patience.

11.2. Soft Skills: The Essential Catalysts

Remarkably, mastering this juggling act isn't entirely reliant on managing external activities. Internally nurturing our emotional intelligence and soft skills significantly enhances our ability to balance these two important aspects of life.

1. Flexibility: Embrace the fact that plans may not always work out as expected. Your ability to adapt to sudden changes increases your success in regulating the balance.

2. Empathy: Understand your child's needs and perspective, alongside understanding your professional obligations. Embracing empathy ensures no sphere feels overlooked.

3. Patience: Juggling professional and parenting roles requires immense patience. Things may not always fall into place, but patience ensures you stay level-headed and calm.

4. Gratitude: Practice gratefulness. Recognizing your blessings greatly improves psychological well-being, thereby inducing more positivity and efficiency in battling daily challenges.

11.3. Celebrating Success: The Imperative Balance

We often associate success with achieving the ultimate. However, in the juggling act of work and parenting, we must understand that success may not always scream grandiose. More often, it's the quiet, steadfast resilience each day, masked by common yet significant victories—submitting work before deadlines, attending your child's soccer game, cooking their favorite meal on a busy day, having an uninterrupted conversation with your partner, or managing some "me" time.

Further, acknowledge the effort that each small accomplishment takes and celebrate it without restraint. These victories unravel the triumphant spirit of an individual who manages to carve success in two demanding aspects—work and parenting.

11.4. The Grand Harmony: Insights

This splendid symphony of work and parenting does not solely lie in muting one segment amidst the loud strains of the other; rather, it manifests in the harmonious co-existence and persistent performance of both sections.

Work doesn't need to overshadow parenting, nor does parenting have to quieten the work. It's a matter of integrating, harmonizing, and tuning them to each other's frequency.

Choosing career aspirations doesn't translate into compromised parenting. Conversely, assuming parenting responsibilities doesn't mean silencing your professional contribution. With tangible strategies, intrinsic motivation, and a relentless spirit, it's possible to enjoy the essence and exploration of both dimensions, creating a beautiful rhythm uniquely yours—a harmony called "life."

The road to achieving balance may be riddled with uncertainties and obstacles. Yet the joy derived from successful parenthood and fulfilling work pursuits will make this journey all the more rewarding and fulfilling. It promises not just fruitful results but also the satisfaction of managing two imperative roles of your life efficiently and effectively—creating a wholesome and enriching life experience. Realize that this balance is not a destination but a continuous journey, made beautiful by your resilience, efforts, and the small victories along the way.